E♭ ALTO SAXOPHONE

FILM FAVORITES

Solos and Band Arrangements
Correlated with Essential Elements® Band Method

Arranged by
MICHAEL SWEENEY, JOHN MOSS and PAUL LAVENDER

Welcome to ESSENTIAL ELEMENTS FILM FAVORITES! The arrangements in this versatile book can be used either in a full concert band setting or as solos for individual instruments. The SOLO pages appear at the beginning of the book, followed by the BAND ARRANGEMENT pages. The supplemental CD recording or PIANO ACCOMPANIMENT book may be used as an accompaniment for solo performance.

ISBN 978-0-634-08694-6

HAL•LEONARD®
CORPORATION
7777 W. BLUEMOUND RD. P.O. BOX 13819 MILWAUKEE, WI 53213

00860146

PIRATES OF THE CARIBBEAN

(A medley including: The Medallion Calls • The Black Pearl)

Eb ALTO SAXOPHONE
Solo

Music by KLAUS BADELT
Arranged by MICHAEL SWEENEY

From the Paramount and Twentieth Century Fox Motion Picture TITANIC

MY HEART WILL GO ON

(Love Theme From 'Titanic')

Eb ALTO SAXOPHONE
Solo

Music by JAMES HORNER
Lyric by WILL JENNINGS
Arranged by JOHN MOSS

00860146

From THE MUPPET MOVIE
THE RAINBOW CONNECTION

Eb ALTO SAXOPHONE
Solo

Words and Music by
PAUL WILLIAMS and KENNETH L. ASCHER
Arranged by PAUL LAVENDER

From THE LORD OF THE RINGS: THE FELLOWSHIP OF THE RING

MAY IT BE

Eb ALTO SAXOPHONE
Solo

**Words and Music by EITHNE NI BHRAONAIN,
NICKY RYAN and ROMA RYAN**
Arranged by JOHN MOSS

00860146

From Walt Disney Pictures' TARZAN™
YOU'LL BE IN MY HEART

Eb ALTO SAXOPHONE
Solo

Words and Music by
PHIL COLLINS
Arranged by MICHAEL SWEENEY

00860146

From the Motion Picture SHREK 2

ACCIDENTALLY IN LOVE

Eb ALTO SAXOPHONE
Solo

Words and Music by
ADAM F. DURITZ
Arranged by MICHAEL SWEENEY

00860146

ALSO SPRACH ZARATHUSTRA

E♭ ALTO SAXOPHONE
Solo

By RICHARD STRAUSS
Arranged by MICHAEL SWEENEY

Broadly

From the Paramount Motion Picture MISSION: IMPOSSIBLE
MISSION: IMPOSSIBLE THEME

E♭ ALTO SAXOPHONE
Solo

By LALO SCHIFRIN
Arranged by MICHAEL SWEENEY

From SHREK

MUSIC FROM SHREK

(A medley including: Fairytale Opening • Ride The Dragon)

Eb ALTO SAXOPHONE
Solo

Music by **JOHN POWELL**
and **HARRY GREGSON-WILLIAMS**
Arranged by JOHN MOSS

From the TriStar Motion Picture THE MASK OF ZORRO

ZORRO'S THEME

E♭ ALTO SAXOPHONE
Solo

**Composed by
JAMES HORNER**
Arranged by JOHN MOSS

PIRATES OF THE CARIBBEAN

(A medley including: The Medallion Calls • The Black Pearl)

E♭ ALTO SAXOPHONE
Band Arrangement

Music by KLAUS BADELT
Arranged by MICHAEL SWEENEY

"The Medallion Calls"
Majestically

* - new note

Optional Faster Tempo "The Black Pearl"

From the Paramount and Twentieth Century Fox Motion Picture TITANIC

MY HEART WILL GO ON

(Love Theme From 'Titanic')

Eb ALTO SAXOPHONE
Band Arrangement

Music by JAMES HORNER
Lyric by WILL JENNINGS
Arranged by JOHN MOSS

00860146

From THE MUPPET MOVIE

THE RAINBOW CONNECTION

E♭ ALTO SAXOPHONE
Band Arrangement

Words and Music by
PAUL WILLIAMS and **KENNETH L. ASCHER**
Arranged by PAUL LAVENDER

00860146

From THE LORD OF THE RINGS: THE FELLOWSHIP OF THE RING

MAY IT BE

Eb ALTO SAXOPHONE
Band Arrangement

**Words and Music by EITHNE NI BHRAONAIN,
NICKY RYAN and ROMA RYAN**

Arranged by JOHN MOSS

00860146

YOU'LL BE IN MY HEART

From Walt Disney Pictures' TARZAN™

E♭ ALTO SAXOPHONE
Band Arrangement

**Words and Music by
PHIL COLLINS**
Arranged by MICHAEL SWEENEY

00860146

From the Motion Picture SHREK 2

ACCIDENTALLY IN LOVE

Eb ALTO SAXOPHONE
Band Arrangement

Words and Music by
ADAM F. DURITZ
Arranged by MICHAEL SWEENEY

00860146

ALSO SPRACH ZARATHUSTRA

By RICHARD STRAUSS
Arranged by MICHAEL SWEENEY

E♭ ALTO SAXOPHONE
Band Arrangement

00860146

From the Paramount Motion Picture MISSION: IMPOSSIBLE

MISSION: IMPOSSIBLE THEME

Eb ALTO SAXOPHONE
Band Arrangement

By LALO SCHIFRIN
Arranged by MICHAEL SWEENEY

From SHREK
MUSIC FROM SHREK
(A medley including: Fairytale Opening • Ride The Dragon)

E♭ ALTO SAXOPHONE
Band Arrangement

Music by JOHN POWELL and HARRY GREGSON-WILLIAMS
Arranged by JOHN MOSS

00860146

From the TriStar Motion Picture THE MASK OF ZORRO

ZORRO'S THEME

E♭ **ALTO SAXOPHONE**
Band Arrangement

Composed by JAMES HORNER
Arranged by JOHN MOSS

Heroically

MORE
FAVORITES FROM
ESSENTIAL ELEMENTS

These superb collections feature favorite songs that students can play as they progress through their band method books. Each song is arranged to be played by either a full band or by individual soloists, with optional accompaniment on CD.

Each song appears twice in the book, featuring:
- Solo instrument version
- Band arrangement for full band or ensembles
- Pop-style accompaniment CD included with conductor's score
- Accompaniment CD available separately
- Piano accompaniment book that is compatible with recorded backgrounds

Prices:
- Conductor Books $29.99
- Instrument Books $8.99
- Piano Accompaniment Books $12.99
- Accompaniment CDs $12.99

Instrument books for each collection feature separate books for the following: Flute, Oboe, Bassoon, B♭ Clarinet, E♭ Alto Clarinet, B♭ Bass Clarinet, E♭ Alto Saxophone, B♭ Tenor Saxophone, E♭ Baritone Saxophone, B♭ Trumpet, F Horn, Trombone, Baritone B.C., Baritone T.C., Tuba, Percussion, and Keyboard Percussion.

BROADWAY FAVORITES
Arranged by Michael Sweeney
Songs include:
Beauty and the Beast
Tomorrow
Cabaret
Edelweiss
Don't Cry for Me Argentina
Get Me to the Church on Time
I Dreamed a Dream
Go Go Go Joseph
Memory
The Phantom of the Opera
Seventy Six Trombones

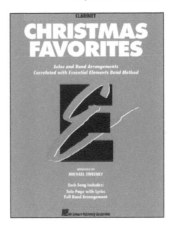

CHRISTMAS FAVORITES
Arranged by Michael Sweeney
Songs include:
The Christmas Song
  (Chestnuts Roasting on an Open Fire)
Frosty the Snow Man
A Holly Jolly Christmas
Jingle-Bell Rock
Let It Snow! Let It Snow! Let It Snow!
Rockin' Around the Christmas Tree
Rudolph, the Red-Nosed Reindeer.

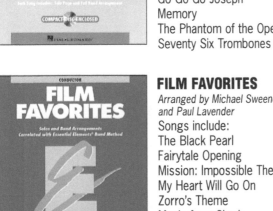

FILM FAVORITES
Arranged by Michael Sweeney, John Moss and Paul Lavender
Songs include:
The Black Pearl
Fairytale Opening
Mission: Impossible Theme
My Heart Will Go On
Zorro's Theme
Music from Shrek
May It Be
The Medallion Calls
You'll Be in My Heart
The Rainbow Connection
Accidentally in Love
Also Sprach Zarathustra

MOVIE FAVORITES
Arranged by Michael Sweeney
Includes themes from:
An American Tail
Back to the Future
Chariots of Fire
Apollo 13
E.T.
Forrest Gump
Dances with Wolves
Jurassic Park
The Man from Snowy River
Raiders of the Lost Ark
Star Trek

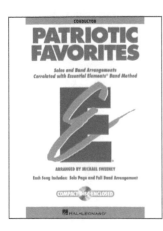

PATRIOTIC FAVORITES
Arranged by Michael Sweeney
Songs include:
America, the Beautiful
Armed Forces Salute
Battle Hymn of the Republic
God Bless America
Hymn to the Fallen
My Country, 'Tis of Thee (America)
The Patriot
The Star Spangled Banner
Stars and Stripes Forever
This Is My Country
Yankee Doodle/Yankee Dookle Boy

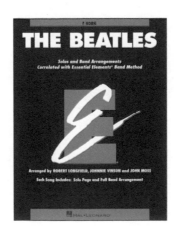

THE BEATLES
Arranged by Robert Longfield, Johnnie Vinson and John Moss
Songs include:
And I Love Her
A Hard Day's Night
Yesterday
Get Back
Lady Madonna
Twist and Shout
Hey Jude
Eleanor Rigby
Ticket to Ride
Here, There and Everywhere
I Want to Hold Your Hand

HAL•LEONARD®
Visit Hal Leonard Online at **www.halleonard.com**

Prices, contents, and availability subject to change without notice.
Some products may not be available outside the U.S.A.